"A Most Important Epocha"
The Coming of the Revolution
in South Carolina

Robert M. Weir

TRICENTENNIAL BOOKLET NUMBER 5

Published for the South Carolina Tricentennial Commission
by the University of South Carolina Press
Columbia, South Carolina

Copyright © 1970 by
The University of South Carolina Press

Published in Columbia, S. C., by
The University of South Carolina Press, 1970

Third Printing 1977

International Standard Book Number: 0-87249-139-0

Library of Congress Catalog Card Number: 79-113807

Manufactured in the United States of America

ROBERT M. WEIR is associate professor of history at the
University of South Carolina.

Contents

"This seems to be designed as a most important Epocha in the History of South Carolina, and from this Day it is no longer to be considered as a Colony but as a State."

—WILLIAM TENNENT (August 5, 1776)

Prologue

About midnight on the night of September 14, 1775, in Charleston, South Carolina, 150 men climbed into boats at Gadsden's wharf. Shoving off, they drifted down the Cooper River on the ebb tide and across the bay where they landed on the north shore of James Island slightly to the west of Fort Johnson. Moving quickly, they neared the fort only to find that the small garrison had fled at their approach. The troops, part of the Second South Carolina Regiment of Foot, then occupied the fort.

Late the next day a man slipped quietly out of the back door of his residence on Meeting Street and furtively made his way to a nearby creek. There he climbed into a small boat which took him to the HMS *Tamar* anchored well out in the harbor. Little he wore or carried—except the great seal of His Majesty's province of South Carolina—revealed who he was, Lord William Campbell, Captain General and Governor in Chief of the colony.

Campbell's flight and the seizure of Fort Johnson by troops operating under the orders of the revolutionary council of safety symbolize the collapse of royal authority and the beginning of the Revolution in South Carolina. But, like all symbols, these events are only an evocative shorthand for a greater and more complex reality. The roots of American rebellion lay far in the past and its ramifications far in the

1

future. To a surprising extent, however, the fundamental changes brought about by the Revolution in South Carolina antedated rather than postdated independence. For the most part, they involved emotions and loyalties, not basic political values or structures. This booklet therefore focuses upon the period from 1763 to 1776 during which South Carolinians became estranged from the British empire.

Chapter I

The Prospering Province

"Few countries have, at any time, exhibited so striking an instance of public and private prosperity as appeared in South Carolina between the years 1725 and 1775."

—David Ramsay (1809)

Colonial South Carolinians were the most improbable of rebels. Living in a weak and prosperous colony, they seemed to have ten reasons not to revolt for every one prompting them to rebel. Under the circumstances, it almost seems, no sane man would have wished or dared to revolt.

At the end of the colonial period South Carolina was militarily a weak colony. Slightly over one hundred years old, it was still sparsely populated. Charleston, the chief port in America south of Philadelphia, actually contained only about thirteen hundred dwellings in 1770. The back country, though no longer the wilderness of a very few years before, remained largely undeveloped. The plantation low country was more thickly settled, but in many areas Negro slaves outnumbered freemen by as much as seven to one. Insurrection was therefore a constant, frightening possibility. Thus, the relatively high population density in the low country actually contributed to its weakness. As a result, South Carolinians had long thought that the colony was incapable of defending itself against the French, the Spanish, and even the Indians.

3

Physical safety appeared to be dependent upon British military power.

Furthermore, no one doubted that in protecting shipments of local products the Royal Navy contributed much to the prosperity that prevailed in South Carolina. By the middle of the eighteenth century, it has been estimated, South Carolinians possessed what may have been the highest economic growth rate of any area in the world, and low-country Carolinians probably enjoyed the highest per capita income in North America. The main support of this phenomenal good fortune was rice. Introduced in the 1690's, the crop flourished in the low country. Rather casually placed on the list of enumerated commodities (those which could be shipped only within the British empire) in 1705, rice soon appeared to outgrow its market. In the 1740's South Carolinians therefore began an intensive search for alternative crops. Experiments by Eliza Lucas and others eventually adapted West Indian methods to the cultivation of indigo in South Carolina. Indigo, it turned out, was an ideal supplement to rice: it could be grown on land not suitable for other staples and, thanks to a generous bounty from the British government for its production, it became an extremely profitable crop. Throughout the remainder of the colonial period, prosperity for nearly everyone prevailed. Only the slaves remained the one great exception to all generalizations about the rest of the population.

For most others, not only prosperity but also an unusual degree of freedom characterized life in South Carolina. Correctly assuming that they were among the freest people in the world, South Carolinians prized their liberty as the "best Birth-right and Inheritance" received from their forefathers. These forefathers were of course Englishmen as well as Carolinians, and the freedom that South Carolinians prized so highly rested on the British tradition of liberty. As British Americans, South Carolinians assumed, they shared all the rights and privileges of Englishmen. Perhaps culturally the most English of all Americans, they were also among the proudest and happiest to be part of the empire. Clearly, their chief blessings — security, wealth, and freedom — all seemed to be the result of being British.

Yet, they were also proud of their own achievements. This pride had a certain bumptious nouveau-riche quality. "This polite and rich Colony," the *South Carolina Gazette* predicted, might well become one of the wealthiest, most sophisticated, and most important in America. Perched on what they considered a westernmost outpost of civilization, South Carolinians enjoyed some of the best race horses, some of the handsomest houses, and one of the most sophisticated cultural scenes in America. On these grounds alone their pride was pardonable. More fundamentally, however, their feeling that they were different—a feeling which has characterized South Carolinians ever since—arose from a realization that they lived in something of a model political community. The standards by which they arrived at this happy conclusion came from what has been termed "country ideology."

An amalgam of ideas and assumptions developed and popularized by members of the English political opposition during the late seventeenth and early eighteenth centuries, country ideology quickly spread throughout the empire. Especially popular with Americans, this ideology served as a source of approved standards of political behavior, something of a contemporary Emily Post of politics. In South Carolina where upward social mobility continually brought

newly rich men into politics, such a set of guidelines was
particularly welcome. Modified to suit their own circumstances, country ideology therefore provided South Carolinians with a political ideal based upon definite assumptions
about the nature of man and society.

The foundation of all their political beliefs was their
attitude toward human nature. They deeply distrusted it. The
daily experiences of life demonstrated that man was unre-
liable, subject to emotions, and motivated by self-interest.
Nevertheless, his capacity for rational action made him more
than a mere animal; therefore freedom, defined as the ability
to act in conformity to the dictates of one's own reason,
was the greatest of human values. As the quality that distin-
guished a man from a beast or a slave, liberty was the source
of human dignity.

Thus, the central problem of human existence was the
maintenance of freedom in the face of the threats posed by
man's own frailties. Unless limits were placed on the exercise
of his passions and his power, life was chaos and liberty
impossible. Above all, perhaps because of constant exposure
to the realities of slavery, the prudent individual resolved
never to allow another man to assume uncontrolled power
over him. Personal independence therefore became a nearly
obsessive concern, and the absolute necessity of maintaining
it meant that the possession of property was essential. Economic independence was considered the bulwark of personal
liberty. The resources of the individual alone, however, were
insufficient to secure the social order necessary to freedom.
Therefore governments have been established to aid him by
protecting his property, his freedom, and his life from the
aggressions of his fellow creatures. When government discharged its responsibility, citizens were obligated to support

and obey it. But when it threatened liberty by exceeding the limits of its authority, the people had not only the right but also the duty to resist.

Frequent recourse to such drastic measures was dangerous, however, because it threatened to create the chaos that governments were instituted to avoid. Therefore continuous and effective checks on the power of government were necessary. Under the English system the constitution was thought to perform this function. To South Carolinians the glory of the British constitutional system was that it included institutional means to limit government and insure as far as was humanly possible that it would act according to the principles which ought to govern it. Because the freedom of a citizen depended upon the security of his property, taxes were considered voluntary though necessary gifts toward the support of government. To make these gifts property holders chose representatives whose primary control over the public purse gave them an effective means to check the power of the executive and obtain redress of grievances. In practice, therefore, the chief historical role of the British House of Commons had been the protection of the people. Considering their own Commons House of Assembly to be a small counterpart, South Carolinians looked upon their local representatives as the natural guardians of the liberties and properties of the people of the colony.

Such important responsibilities required a man who was able, independent, courageous, virtuous, and public-spirited. Although riches did not insure that he would exhibit these qualities, it was assumed that they made it more likely. Economic independence promoted courage and material possessions fostered rational behavior. Moreover, wealth enabled him to acquire the education believed necessary for statecraft,

and a large stake in society tied his interest to the welfare of
the whole. Thus a series of interrelated assumptions helped
to maintain a belief that members of a social and economic
elite should rule.

Nevertheless, no matter how qualified and how public-
spirited an individual might seem, appearances could be
deceiving and human nature was prone to corruption. Constituents therefore needed to retain checks upon their representatives. The most effective means was thought to be
harnessing his own self-interests to theirs by making sure that
he held property where they did. Over a period of time,
however, the interests of a representative and his constituent
might diverge; frequent elections were necessary to keep
them aligned. Moreover, without free elections the entire
process of representation was clearly a sham.

Other checks—in addition to those the people maintained
over their representatives—were also thought to be necessary
if government was to perform its proper functions. Collective
bodies of men, like individuals, were apt to be misled by passions, ignorance, and self-interest. Therefore no one branch
of government should dominate the others. "Balanced government"—an equilibrium of power between the executive,
the upper house, and the lower house—was the theoretical
ideal. Historically, the threats to this equilibrium appeared
to come chiefly from the executive who was apt to be cor-
rupted by the daily exercise of power. As a result, it was
deemed necessary for the other branches of government to
be especially vigilant in maintaining their own prerogatives.
Parties or factions, by definition combinations of men acting
together for selfish purposes, were dangerous, not only because they might permit private interests to flourish at the
expense of the public but also, even more importantly, be-

cause they offered an opportunity for the executive to build up centers of support in the other branches of government, thereby weakening their will and subverting their ability to check encroachments of executive power. Consequently the idealized political figure was the individual patriot who exhibited his disinterested concern for the public welfare by rejecting factional ties.

To an amazing extent at mid-century political life in the colony actually conformed to the theoretical ideal. By law South Carolinians went to the polls at least every three years to elect representatives to the Commons House of Assembly. Almost every white adult male found the franchise open to him and, when he voted, he was proud to be one of the few men in the world at the time who could use the secret ballot. Legally his choice of representatives was restricted to men who owned at least five hundred acres and ten slaves or the equivalent in town property. But because the average voter shared the common assumptions about the virtues of property, he generally elected men whose wealth exceeded the necessary minimums. Usually, though not always, the choice proved to be a good one. By the end of the colonial period members of the local elite were often remarkably public-spirited men who sacrificed their time and energy in discharging duties which brought them no financial compensation. Rather, as one contemporary put it, their only rewards were "esteem, admiration, or fame." As Lieutenant Governor William Bull, Jr., noted, the prevailing desire to demonstrate a sense of public responsibility prompted much unpaid voluntary public service of other kinds. Historians have also found that the same desire helped to make the South Carolina Commons perhaps the hardest working lower house in the colonies. Moreover, its members represented a society

with remarkably homogeneous economic interests and cultural values; by and large, groups not sharing this homo-
geneity were not represented. These conditions meant that it
was relatively easy for politicians to heed the imperative to
shun parties and factions. As a result, by mid-century the
South Carolina Commons, unlike most colonial assemblies,
was virtually free of factionalism.

Instead, members of the Commons united in supporting
its rights and privileges at the expense of the other two
branches of the legislature. This "quest for power," was not
unique to South Carolina but it was unusually successful,
and by the end of the colonial period, the South Carolina
Commons was one of the most powerful lower houses in the
colonies. Several factors help to account for its restless ag-
gressiveness: the example of the British House of Commons
in the seventeenth century, the apparently universal tendency
of institutions to aggrandize themselves when unchecked by
other forces, the suspicion of executive power inculcated by
country ideology, and an ever-present uneasiness resulting
from the colonial condition.

Because South Carolina was a colony, the representatives
of the people labored under special disadvantages. Unlike
the British House of Lords, the provincial royal Council,
which served as the upper house of the legislature, did not
represent a separate stratum of society, such as the nobility.
Rather, like the royal governor, its members were appointed
at the pleasure of the Crown. This fact made South Carolinians suspect that the Council was not a truly independent
upper house but an appendage of the executive. The Commons therefore felt outnumbered; it seemed to confront not
one but the combined weight of two other branches of government. Indeed, the odds against the house appeared to be

even higher; in many areas of concern to Americans imperial officials possessed the final authority.

The heart of the empire was London. There an advisory body, the Board of Trade, formulated policy for the colonies and submitted recommendations to other officers such as the secretary of state in whose sphere of responsibility the colonies lay. Ultimately authority for executive action affecting the colonies came from the King in Council; legislative action from Parliament. Consequently all colonies maintained agents —or lobbyists—to speak for them in London. Unfortunately, however, the agents could speak in only a small voice and the authorities did not always choose to hear.

Yet until the 1760's, except for the few men whose nagging worries helped to propel the Commons' aggressive drive for power, South Carolinians hardly realized that the structure of imperial government could place them at the mercy of powers beyond their control. During the first half of the eighteenth century London largely left the colonies alone; and without its active assistance, the governor and Council were obviously no match for a lower house in control of the public purse. As a result, South Carolinians seldom found much need for serious thought about the nature of the imperial constitution. But at the end of the French and Indian War, that changed.

Chapter II

The Stamp Act Crisis

"LIBERTY and PROPERTY, and NO STAMPS"
—Motto of the *South Carolina Gazette and Country Journal* (1765)

The French and Indian War brought momentous changes to the empire. At the Peace of Paris in 1763 Great Britain acquired from France trophies which included Canada and most of Louisiana. From Spain Britain also obtained the Floridas. In fact, Britain virtually ousted its rivals from the North American continent. But success contained the seeds of trouble. Even for the victor, the war had been expensive, and by 1763 the British national debt stood at more than £130,000,000 sterling—a previously unheard of figure. Moreover, the mere increase in the area of the empire presented imperial authorities with new and difficult problems. For solutions they naturally turned toward America.

General attempts to tighten up the old colonial system and drastic innovations in imperial policy toward the colonies followed. Somewhere along the line, imperial authorities assumed (without ever really examining the decision) that a permanent standing army should be stationed in North America; presumably a larger empire needed a larger peacetime army and that seemed like a good place to put much of it. Such an assumption alone represented an important departure from past policy. But even more radical was the decision to have Americans support that army. Prior to this time Parliament had imposed duties on colonial trade merely for the purpose of regulating it, not for revenue. Discovering that the colonial customs service had cost more to maintain than it collected, Chancellor of the Exchequer George Grenville resolved to change matters. As a result, he established stricter controls over colonial shipping, provided more rigorous methods of enforcing the acts of trade, and improved the efficiency of the customs service. Most important, he also induced Parliament to tax the colonies.

Although the preamble of the Sugar Act clearly stated that it was intended "for defraying the expenses of defending, protecting, and securing" His Majesty's dominions in America, South Carolinians failed to heed the warning. Seldom directly interested in the sugar trade, they could not decide how the act would affect them. As a result, unlike New Englanders, they were slow to become upset over the new statute. Incidentally, the same can be said about many measures which contributed heavily to discontent in other colonies. Although they shared many common grievances with other Americans and doubtless would not have revolted except as part of a common cause, South Carolinians had their own problems and their own reasons for rebellion.

At the moment they were still disturbed over Governor Thomas Boone's attempt to challenge the right of the Commons House to determine the validity of the election of its own members. The English House of Commons had exercised this right since the early seventeenth century; the South Carolina Commons claimed it from at least the 1690's. But in the spring of 1762 Boone refused to recognize the election of Christopher Gadsden because the church wardens of St. Paul's Parish, who had supervised the election, had not taken the oath required by law. Gadsden, however, had been the

overwhelming choice of the voters. The Commons therefore
chose to overlook the technical flaw in his election and declared him elected. Boone then precipitously dissolved the
house. Upon meeting, the newly elected Commons censured
Boone and resolved that it alone possessed the right to judge
the qualifications of its own members. Refusing to make concessions, the governor countered by contending that, because
the house owed its existence to the election act, the law ought
to be scrupulously observed. The Commons replied by vigorously contending that its existence depended not on the
election act but upon the natural right of freemen to be
represented. And in mid-December 1762 it refused to do any
further business with Boone until he apologized.

The stalemate continued for more than a year while both
parties tried to secure the support of imperial authorities.
In May 1763 Boone gave up the fight and sailed for England
and Lieutenant Governor William Bull, Jr., took over the
government. The Board of Trade, concluding that Boone
appeared "to have taken up the matter in dispute with more
Zeal than prudence," replaced him as governor. But the
Commons, the Board also found, acted too hastily. Nevertheless, it seemed that the Commons had won a clear-cut victory.

In part because of this victory, the dispute proved to have
wider significance. Undoubtedly, it served as a training
ground for the young politicians, like Gadsden, who were to
lead South Carolina through the rest of the colonial period.
Moreover, success gave them self-confidence. Most important,
the dispute also forced men to clarify their ideas about the
basis and purpose of representation in the colonial assembly.
And with Gadsden they overwhelmingly concluded that liberty in South Carolina depended upon the possession of "a
free assembly, *freely* representing a *free people.*"

Unlike the Sugar Act, the Stamp Act appeared to pose a clear danger to that freedom. Informed in 1764 that the measure was pending, the provincial Commons ordered its agent in London, Charles Garth, "to make all opposition you possibly can, . . . in the laying a stamp duty, or any other tax by act of Parliament on the colonies." The chief reason for opposing the act, Garth was told in no uncertain terms, was "its inconsistency with that inherent right of every British subject, not to be taxed but by his own consent, or that of his representative." Despite the strong words, it is highly probable that many South Carolinians had not yet fully made up their minds about the constitutional questions involved. Direct internal taxation of the colonies by Parliament was a new possibility, obviously unwelcome, probably burdensome, and possibly unconstitutional. At this time Carolinians were not ready to stake opposition to the act upon the uncompromisable grounds of absolue principle; in fact, they explicitly declared that South Carolina would "submit most dutifully at all times to Acts of Parliament."

Parliament refused to accept the validity of American arguments and, in March 1765, passed the Stamp Act. Beginning November 1, 1765, it stipulated that Americans were to pay a tax of varying size upon a wide variety of official and unofficial papers—including playing cards, legal papers, and newspaper advertisements. The year's delay in adopting the act and the further delay of six months before it went into effect permitted and encouraged Americans to make up their minds about the constitutional questions involved. And, as they did so, they took an increasingly firm stand. The most vocal examination of constitutional principles occurred northward of South Carolina. Daniel Dulany of Maryland exploded the British contention that Americans enjoyed "virtual repre-

sentation" by showing that members of the British House of
Commons lacked the most basic qualification of representatives for America, identical interests with their constituents.
The Virginia House of Burgesses passed vigorous resolutions
denouncing the Stamp Act. And on June 8, 1765, the Massachusetts House of Representatives invited all the American
colonies to send representatives to a meeting to be held in
New York the following October.

News of these developments reached South Carolinians
by way of the *South Carolina Gazette,* a newspaper published
in Charleston by Peter Timothy. As one stamp distributor
noted, the colonial printers *"stuffed* their Papers with the
most inflamatory Pieces they could procure." Timothy was
no exception, and Lieutenant Governor Bull termed his paper
the "conduit Pipe" for northern propaganda which, he believed, "poisoned" the minds of South Carolinians with
"principles . . . inbibed and propagated from Boston and
Rhode Island." Bull exaggerated. What came from the northward was not the principles but the willingness to use violence in their defense. For the time being, however, most
South Carolinians shared the point of view held by Henry
Laurens, a rich and influential merchant, who opposed the
act but saw only two alternatives: obedience until the law
could be repealed or "to beat to Arms." "I defy," he added,
"all the grumbletonians from Quebec to West Florida to
point out a medium."

South Carolinians therefore first tried peaceful protest by
sending three delegates to the Stamp Act Congress, Thomas
Lynch, Christopher Gadsden, and John Rutledge. Rutledge,
the youngest at twenty-six, was well on his way to becoming
the leading lawyer in Charleston; Lynch had a reputation
for being a "solid, firm, judicious man." And Gadsden was

an indefatigable, public-spirited zealot who with pardonable pride could later claim that "no man in America strove more (and more successfully) first to bring about a Congress in 1765, and then to support it afterwards than myself." Meeting in New York in early October, delegates from the American colonies hammered out fourteen declarations "respecting the most Essential Rights and Liberties of the Colonists, and of the Grievances under which they labour, by Reason of several late Acts of Parliament." An address to the king and petitions to both houses of Parliament followed.

In the meantime, events in South Carolina moved rapidly. The triennial election for the Commons House occurred in early October, and as one observer remarked, "the minds of the freeholders were inflamed . . . by many a hearty damn of the Stamp act over bottles, bowls and glasses." By October 18, South Carolinians were accordingly prepared for the arrival of the *Planters Adventure* when, with stamps aboard, it anchored under the protecting guns of Fort Johnson. Early the following morning a gallows forty feet high appeared in the center of Charleston; hanging from it was an effigy of a stamp distributor. Powerless to maintain order, royal officials could only stand aside that evening as a crowd of about two thousand persons carried the effigy eastward along Broad Street to the bay. Along the way the procession passed the home of George Saxby, the inspector of stamps, who had not yet returned from London. Rifling his house, the crowd then continued on to an open spot where it burned the effigy and buried a coffin labeled "American Liberty." Before dispersing, the mob also broke into and searched Caleb Lloyd's house on a rumor that he had been appointed stamp distributor. Having escaped earlier, he was nowhere to be found, nor did he make an appearance for more than a week. Similar

disorders occurred the following day. Lieutenent Governor
Bull therefore ordered the stamps secretly transferred from
the *Planters Adventure* to Fort Johnson. Even there they
were not safe, and Bull next ordered them moved to HMS
Speedwell out in the harbor.

Not surprisingly, when emissaries from the mob visited
Saxby and Lloyd to demand that they resign their offices,
they hesitated only a short while. The Sons of Liberty had
insured that no stamps would be available on November 1,
the day that the act was to take effect. As a result, the customs house serving the port closed down; and business came
to a halt in all the civil courts.

The port presented the most serious difficulty. During the
late fall and winter South Carolina normally exported the
rice crop. Vessels expecting to load therefore arrived to find
that they were unable to depart without legal clearances
which could not be obtained. By the end of December vessels
packed the harbor; barrels of rice crammed the wharves and
warehouses of Charleston; and idle sailors thronged the
streets and taverns. Only the pockets of local merchants and
planters were empty. Clearly the embargo jeopardized the
peace and safety, as well as the economy, of the colony. As
a result, considerable pressure developed to permit the use of
stamps. But Gadsden, who had returned from the meeting of
the Stamp Act Congress, strove with the help of the Sons of
Liberty to infuse some of his own resolution into others. They
and their posterity, he declared, would be "made happy in
the preservation of their and our just rights and privileges,
whether they will or no." His tactics worked.

In the meantime the newly elected Commons House met,
approved the actions of the Stamp Act Congress, and passed
a series of resolutions similar to the declarations adopted at

New York. Significantly, these resolutions omitted the phrase by which the Stamp Act Congress acknowledged "due subordination" of the colonies to Parliament. Instead, the Commons told its agent, Garth, that "in taxing ourselves and making Laws for our own internal government or police we can by no means allow our Provincial legislatures to be subordinate to any legislative power on earth." Moreover, the members arranged to have their proceedings published in a local newspaper so that their "Sense of Liberty" and loyalty might "be known to their Constituents, and transmitted to Posterity."

By January 1766 nearly everyone's nerves were on edge over the embargo at the port. And among the most impatient individuals were the idle English sailors. At first the Sons of Liberty had hoped by tying up ships in Charleston to induce British merchants to petition the government to repeal the Stamp Act. But nearly fourteen hundred restive seamen caused a change in plans. Fearing that the sailors might be able to compel local officials to use the stamps, Gadsden and the Sons of Liberty made a tactical retreat to save a strategic victory. Late in December and early in January a number of the largest vessels in the harbor from home ports in Great Britain quietly cleared and sailed. With them went large crews. In all probability the Sons of Liberty issued their own special "clearances" which permitted the use of stamped paper.

By the end of January a crisis was clearly at hand; unless either the Sons of Liberty or royal officials gave in and permitted vessels to clear regularly, with or without stamps, widespread violence appeared inevitable. Under tremendous pressure from the Commons House and the merchant community, Lieutenant Governor Bull finally capitulated, and

on February 3 he began to issue certificates stating that no
stamped paper was available. Customs officials then permitted vessels to clear on the basis of these documents. Bull's
assessment of the situation explained his conduct. Any attempt to enforce the act before the king had considered the
petitions against it, he told imperial authorities, would "oc-
casion much confusion and some bloodshed, and will not in
all human probability establish the regular Execution of the
Act." Violence obviously had its uses.

It was, however, an inappropriate device for opening the
courts where the resumption of business depended as much
upon the willingness of local lawyers to violate the letter of
the law as it did upon the cooperativeness of royal officials.
Lawyers being conservative by training, if not by tempera-
ment, this willingness developed slowly. Nevertheless by
January 22, a delegation from the local bar asked Chief Justice Charles Shinner to open the court of common pleas.
Thrown into a quandry by the need to make a decision, Shinner stalled and then decided that no business would be con-
ducted in the court of common pleas in violation of the
Stamp Act.

The chief justice therefore proved to be an almost insur-
mountable obstacle to the normal functioning of the courts,
though Lieutenant Governor Bull was a party to attempts at
circumventing him. Responding to a suggestion of the lawyers, Bull appointed three new assistant judges: Rawlins
Lowndes, Benjamin Smith, and Daniel Doyley. When the
court met on April 1, Lowndes spoke for the assistant judges.
Could Parliament, he asked, have intended "by this Law to
Abrogate and repeal all precedent Acts of Parliament, to
unhinge the Constitution of the Colonies, to unloose the
hands of Violence and Oppression, to introduce Anarchy

and Confusion amongst us, and to reduce us to a State of
Outlawry?" Obviously not, yet such appeared to be the result of closing the court. Clearly, therefore, the act should
not be construed to require that all legal business be suspended merely because stamped paper was unavailable.
Whatever the cause, "impossibilities," he declared, "are still
impossibilities." The present situation was "as much to be
attributed to the Act of God, as if the Ship which brought
them [the stamped papers] into the Province had been cast
away in a Storm, for nothing less than his immediate and
irresistable influence could have as it were in a Moment
united all America and made them as the heart of one Man."

Unimpressed by this ingenious reasoning, Shinner and
the clerk of the court, Dougal Campbell, refused to cooperate. The other judges, later joined by the Commons,
then attempted to have Campbell removed from his office,
but the arrival of unofficial news that the Stamp Act had
been repealed saved him. But Shinner, who was an incred-
ibly stubborn man, still refused to do any business until he
received official notice of the repeal. The Commons, having
lost patience, then turned its attention to removing him. Unlike Campbell, Shinner was incompetent, and it was not difficult to assemble a damning indictment. Suspended from
his office by the new governor, Lord Charles Montagu, Shinner died while his case was being appealed through the
hierarchy of imperial authorities. Though well-intentioned,
Shinner was not intelligent enough to see when the situation
required flexibility, and there is no question but that he
unnecessarily prolonged the crisis.

Contemporary South Carolinians, however, tended to overlook his sins in their joy at the repeal of the Stamp Act.
Early in March 1766, colonial unrest, pressure by British

merchants, and a new ministry combined to bring about repeal. But news of the action did not reach Charleston until
May 3. When it did, Charlestonians celebrated the day with
a parade by local military units and illuminated the night
by placing candles in their windows. The Commons asked
the delegates to the Stamp Act Congress to sit for portraits
to hang in the State House "as a memorial of the high esteem
this House have for their Persons and merit, and the great
service they have done their Country." The house also resolved to erect a statue to William Pitt as a tribute "for his
noble, Disinterested, and Generous Assistance . . . towards
obtaining the Repeal of the Stamp Act." Moreover, by happy
coincidence, the day on which an official copy of the repeal
act arrived, June 4, was the king's birthday. The result was
a holiday such as Charleston had seldom seen. Colors
streamed from all the ships in the harbor; church bells
rang; the governor, councillors, house members, and public
officers reviewed the Charleston militia companies as they
paraded down Broad Street; at noon the cannon at the forts
boomed out salutes, and in the evening Lieutenant Governor
Bull entertained the reviewing party at Dillon's Tavern. It
was a gala day marred only by bad weather which prevented
many events scheduled for the evening.

Superstitious persons might also have detected ominous
portents in the political weather. The Stamp Act crisis had
brought many of the American colonies, including South
Carolina, to the very brink of rebellion. Faced with direct
internal taxation by Parliament, Americans reasoned that if
they submitted, they would establish a precedent which
could place their property at the mercy of men beyond
their control. In the future, they thought it only reasonable
to suppose, imperial authorities would find it expedient to

shift the burden of taxation from their own constituents to those who had no recourse. As one South Carolinian put it, Americans were like unbroken donkeys, if they accepted this measure, *"more Sacks, more Sacks"* were coming. What these sacks might contain was what worried them.

Unable to prevent enforcement of the act in any other way, Americans turned to violence. It proved successful, and a number of implications followed. Perhaps most important, resistance to British authority appeared to become a real option. Understanding this, many British politicians considered repeal of the Stamp Act to be a mistake. To placate those British politicians repeal was coupled with passage of the Declaratory Act which stated that Parliament possessed the right to legislate for the colonies "in all cases whatsoever." Yet only a few months before the South Carolina Commons had told Garth that, as far as local affairs were concerned, South Carolinians could permit their own assembly to be "subordinate to no power on earth." Many Americans erroneously thought that repeal of the Stamp Act meant that British authorities had accepted their point of view. Thus the Declaratory Act appeared to be, in the words of Henry Laurens, only "the last feeble struggle of the Grenvillian party." Such optimism was misguided and, as Laurens later realized, the principles of the Declaratory Act would eventually make a "platform for the Invincible Reasoning from the Mouths of four and twenty pounders." Cannon would ultimately decide the issue, but in 1766 only a few die-hards like Gadsden, who harangued the Sons of Liberty in the shade of the Liberty Tree about the threat posed by the Declaratory Act, recognized the dangers.

Nevertheless, the emotional impact of the Stamp Act crisis seriously endangered the empire. Thereafter, imperial officials occasionally suspected that Americans were conspiring among themselves to throw off British control. Americans often suspected that imperial authorities were conspiring to enslave them. But if the Stamp Act crisis drove a wedge between Great Britain and America, it also helped to cement a union between the American colonies. Drawn together by the common threat to all, their leaders recognized that there was safety in numbers. As Gadsden put it, in the crisis there should be "no New England men, no New Yorker, etc., known on the Continent, but all of us Americans." Corresponding and meeting with each other, especially in the Stamp Act Congress, Americans laid the foundations of the American union. Indeed, they turned March 18, the day the act was repealed, into a national holiday before they were a nation.

Chapter III

Customs Racketeering

"In time such Evils, if not suppressed, will work an alienation of American Subjects from the Mother Country and perhaps mark a fatal line of separation between the two Countries."
                                                        —Henry Laurens (1769)

The next upheaval after the Stamp Act crisis began in the spring of 1767 when a new customs collector, Daniel Moore, arrived in Charleston. Moore had been a member of Parliament, and he may have come to his new position thoroughly imbued with patriotic zeal to tighten up the customs service. If so, he came to the wrong place, since South Carolina had never been a smugglers' haven. It is considerably more likely that Moore arrived intending to make his fortune at the expense of South Carolinians. If so, he also came to the wrong place, for they proved uncooperative.

At any rate, whenever it benefitted him financially, Moore began to enforce existing trade regulations so strictly that he himself violated the spirit, if not the letter, of the law. Enraged merchants responded in the local courts with an avalanche·of suits and complaints against him. Within six months of his arrival, Moore fled to England, but not before his actions precipitated one of the most notorious incidents of the whole pre-Revolutionary period in South Carolina.

Apparently wishing to make an example of a leading local merchant, Moore ordered his henchmen to seize two

25

schooners belonging to Henry Laurens. Both vessels had
made the round trip between Charleston and Laurens' property in Georgia. In theory, coasting vessels engaged in inter-
colonial trade were supposed to clear each voyage with the
customs service, but because there was no customs house near
his plantation Laurens had not cleared these vessels precisely
as required. Normally, in such cases officials overlooked the
letter of the law. Moore refused to do so, and the vessels
came to trial in the court of vice-admiralty. Because of the
specialized nature of admiralty law, this court functioned
without a jury, the judge making all the decisions himself.
At this time the judge was Egerton Leigh, a connection by
marriage and close personal friend of Laurens. Offsetting
these ties, however, was Leigh's desire to protect his own
position. Taking advantage of a technicality, he therefore
attempted to arrange a compromise by ordering one of the
vessels forfeited and the other one returned to Laurens.
Moreover, Leigh neglected to declare that reasonable grounds
existed for believing that the discharged schooner had been
operating in violation of the law. The omission opened the
way for Laurens to recover his losses on the one vessel by
suing for damages in the case of the other.

Leigh's attempt at compromise only compounded the difficulties. Laurens sued George Roupell, the customs searcher
who had made the actual seizure, and the jury awarded
Laurens a judgment which Roupell was unable to pay. Roupell was therefore in danger of going to jail. To rescue him
from his predicament the new customs collector, R. P. H.
Hatley, then deliberately delayed receiving the required bond
for goods already aboard the *Ann*, a large vessel belonging
partly to Laurens, so that Roupell could seize it. Acting
through intermediaries, Roupell then offered to release the

ship if Laurens would surrender his demand for damages. Laurens refused, and the case went before the court of vice-admiralty, where Judge Leigh found himself upon the horns of a dilemma. On the one hand, because local customs officials had been filing a steady stream of complaints against him, he could not hope to retain his office unless he protected Roupell. On the other hand, because customs officers had obviously resorted to subterfuge, it was extremely difficult to shield them from another suit. Leigh solved the problem by forcing Roupell to take the seldom used oath of calumny, a declaration that his actions had not been motivated by malice. The bond had not been posted; the vessel was technically in violation of the law; Roupell swore that he had acted in good faith; ipso facto there was a probable cause of seizure, and Leigh so certified when he discharged the vessel, noting that he had a "Strong Suspicion that there was more of design and Surprise on the part of some officers than of any intention to commit fraud on the part of the Claimant."

Considering the pressures upon him, Leigh's decision was reasonably fair, but it made him vulnerable. Roupell complained to his superiors that "no Judge of Admiralty can make a Court of Equity of it upon all occasions, which for this year past has been the case." Laurens, who was understandably filled with righteous rage at the treatment he had received, pilloried Leigh in a pamphlet entitled *Extracts from the Proceedings of the Court of Vice-Admiralty*. Leigh defended himself with *The Man Unmasked*. Laurens replied with an amplified version of the *Extracts*. Leigh's polemics were largely a personal attack, but Laurens was able to give his pamphlets wide distribution and wider significance by showing that the customs officials had been guilty of grossly

abusing their powers. Moreover, he clearly demonstrated
that Leigh had placed his own self-interest above his duty
to curb them. By permitting men like Leigh to render such
decisions, unchecked by a jury or other judges, Laurens contended, the admiralty courts put American merchants at the
mercy of one man who might be "a fool or a knave or both."
Since passage of the Sugar and Stamp acts—revenue acts that
were enforceable in the vice-admiralty courts—the courts
had become increasingly unpopular with Americans who
attacked their jurisdiction on the ground that it deprived
colonials of the basic right to trial by a jury of their peers.
Coincidentally, at almost the same time that Laurens was
undergoing his ordeal, John Hancock was having similar and
widely publicized experiences in Boston. Although Hancock
probably helped to bring his troubles upon himself, there is
considerable evidence to indicate that many customs officials
did attempt a kind of racketeering at the expense of Americans. Laurens' pamphlets therefore found a receptive audi-
ence throughout America.

As a result of the controversy, Leigh lost his judicial post
and much prestige. Henry Laurens, who had been rather
lukewarm before, became an ardent champion of American
rights and a popular figure throughout the colonies. Furthermore, many Americans came to take a more jaundiced view
of the customs service and the admiralty courts. And perhaps
equally important in the short run, South Carolinians began
to grow impatient with the caliber of royal officials sent to
the colony. Although Chief Justice Shinner could be written
off as an honest mistake, Moore and Leigh made many Carolinians wonder if imperial authorities had not unleashed a
flock of harpies upon them.

Chapter IV

Discontent in the Back Country

"Perhaps the orders for limiting the number of members are as *peculiar* as any that have been given on the continent."
—John MacKenzie (1768)

While Laurens was having difficulties with admiralty affairs the province as a whole was having even more serious problems over conditions in the back country. Following the French and Indian War immigrants from the north, many of them Scotch-Irish, surged into the middle and western portions of the province. By the mid-1760's these settlers probably numbered more than thirty thousand. But at the end of the Cherokee War in 1762 much of the back country resembled, as one historian has put it, "a huge disaster area." Not only were many of the settlements devastated but the war demoralized the populace. As a result, by the mid-1760's, bands of outlaws roamed through the area stealing, raping, and killing. To combat these evils, law-abiding citizens organized themselves as vigilantes to "regulate" the outlaws. But other problems, less amenable to such solutions, also existed. Schools were virtually non-existent; dissenting churches scarce and the tax-supported Anglican churches of the low country practically inaccessible. The same was true of the civil and criminal courts which were held only at Charleston. All in all, back-country men had a tendency to believe that the only men connected with the government who realized that they existed were the tax collectors. The

29

root of the trouble appeared to be lack of representation in the assembly which prevented back-country men from effectively bringing their needs to the attention of government.

A substantial part of the difficulty arose from conditions imposed by imperial authorities who had resolved, if possible, to check the rising power of the colonial houses of assembly. One means might be to limit their size. Thus the royal governor in South Carolina received instructions not to approve any legislation adding representatives to the Commons. Extending more adequate representation to the back country therefore meant taking seats away from established parishes. Needless to say, the back country continued to be under-represented. Quite willing to acknowledge the justice of its claim to representation, men such as the low-country planter John MacKenzie could not help but feel that the instruction limiting the size of the colonial assemblies was one of the most *"peculiar"* ever issued.

A similar problem confronted the assembly when it attempted to provide circuit courts for the back country. In England since the early eighteenth century judges possessed tenure during "good behavior." In America they were removable at the will of the Crown. Attempts to obtain equal treatment for American judges had provoked disputes in other colonies, most notably New York. In South Carolina the issue was not one of great importance until local leaders filled the assistant judgeships during the Stamp Act crisis. But in 1768, while drafting a bill to provide courts for the back country, the Commons undertook to protect the incumbent judges as well as to establish a principle by stipulating that local judges should hold their offices during good behavior. For this and other reasons imperial authorities disallowed the law. Realizing that courts were desperately needed, the Commons then abandoned the contest in order to prevent further delays. Although some of its members later deeply regretted the action, their willingness to accept the conditions imposed by London demonstrated their sensitivity to the problems of the back country.

The aftermath of the affair was unfortunate. Because Lieutenant Governor Bull felt that finding qualified Carolinians willing to accept the new judgeships would be difficult, he recommended that second-rate English lawyers be appointed. As a result, British placemen gradually replaced the temporary American incumbents. Friction between the new judges and local leaders followed. Resentment by the latter at what they took to be an insult to themselves and a snub to American rights caused part of the difficulty, but another issue also contributed. Some of the first cases over which the new judges presided involved Regulator activities. Rawlins Lowndes and the other colonial judges approached these cases as politicians rather than judges. Willing to forget the letter of the law, they believed "that a veil should be drawn over these unhappy transactions." Unfamiliar with local conditions, the new English judges were appalled by this homespun and common-sense approach to justice. Many South Carolinians were equally appalled at the officious arrogance of the new judges. In fact, it seemed that whenever imperial authorities or their minions interfered in South Carolina they made a mess of things. Conditions in the back country had approached anarchy. Why? To many local leaders the answer seemed to be because British authorities imposed conditions which made it impossible to solve local problems without sacrificing basic colonial rights. This reasoning was not entirely fair, but emotion warped logic. Increasingly, the process jeopardized the future of the empire.

Chapter V

Non-Importation

"The monstrous and slavish doctrine of *trusting* to the British parliament to do us justice . . . absolutely comprehends every species of the most abject slavery."

—A "Resolutionist" (1770)

Meanwhile, another crisis was developing. In the spring of 1767, Charles Townshend, chancellor of the exchequer in the Chatham ministry, resolved once again to extract revenue from the recalcitrant Americans. They appeared to make a distinction between external and internal taxation. Well, if so, he would humor them though he himself saw no logical distinction between the two forms of taxation. Neither did Americans, but Townshend died before he realized the full extent of his mistake. At any rate, Parliament passed the new revenue measure in June, stipulating that it would become effective November 20, 1767. Duties were to be collected upon all glass, lead, paint, paper, and tea imported into America. The proceeds, expected to be about forty thousand pounds per year, were to be applied to the costs not only of defending but also of governing the colonies. In other words, the intention was to make royal officials as financially independent of the local assemblies as possible. Moreover, in an attempt to insure efficient collection of the new duties the act established new vice-admiralty courts and a special board of customs commissioners with headquarters at Boston.

Predictably, opposition to the measure first developed in

Massachusetts. On October 28, the Boston town meeting attempted to pressure British merchants into working for repeal of the new duties by urging individuals not to import specified British goods. The non-importation movement soon spread to other cities in New England and the middle colonies, where John Dickinson composed his famous series of essays, *Letters From A Farmer In Pennsylvania*. Widely circulated throughout the colonies, including South Carolina, these essays argued that a tax was a tax though it might be disguised as a duty. Duties to regulate trade within the empire were perfectly permissible; taxation without representation was unconstitutional. Sharing this point of view, the Massachusetts House of Representatives in February 1768 addressed a circular letter to the assemblies of the other American colonies urging joint action to oppose the Townshend Act. The governor of Massachusetts responded by dissolving the house; Secretary of State Hillsborough ordered that the next house also be dissolved if it refused to rescind the letter and that other colonial governors dissolve their assemblies if necessary to prevent them from considering the Massachusetts circular. Meanwhile John Hancock's difficulties with the customs officials led to violence; the officials fled to the fort in the harbor; and by October 1, 1768, British troops moved into Boston to maintain order and support royal authority.

When not occupied with their own problems of extortion in the customs service and lawlessness in the back country, South Carolinians took a keen interest in what was happening in the north. Perhaps in part attempting to excuse the behavior of his neighbors, Lieutenant Governor Bull unhappily reported, "We are too apt to cast our eyes to the North Star of Boston in our Political Navigation." When the

Commons met in November 1768, Governor Montagu told
its members that he hoped that they would treat with the
"contempt it deserves" any letter they might receive advo-
cating unwarranted combinations against the authority of
king and Parliament. While the house was not in session
its speaker, Peter Manigault, had received the Massachusetts
circular, which he promptly referred to the Commons for
consideration. Unanimously endorsing the circular, the house
solemnly assured Montagu that it had received no communi-
cation challenging the just authority of Parliament. Enraged,
Montagu dissolved it. Thus Hillsborough's instructions to
dissolve the assemblies if they proved obstreperous helped
to prevent another meeting like the Stamp Act Congress, but
narrowing the available options undoubtedly made Americans more willing to adopt non-importation.

Nevertheless, most Americans—including South Carolinians—took the step reluctantly. To inconvenience British
merchants they had to inconvenience themselves. This was
bad enough, but an even greater obstacle to the movement
for non-importation was the jealousy that it engendered
among unequally affected economic groups. Commercial im-
porters of British goods might be ruined by a general agreement not to purchase their wares, while the more self-suffi-
cient planters might hardly feel the sacrifice. Local artisans,
whose handiwork sometimes competed with British products,
could even benefit.

In South Carolina a good deal of pulling and hauling
between the three interested groups was necessary before a
reasonably satisfactory arrangement could be worked out.
In the end, however, planters, who were collectively the
most potent numerical and economic group, emerged with
the decisive voice in the matter.

During June 1769 a series of letters urging vigorous action appeared in the *South-Carolina Gazette*. One of them dated from the Pedee and signed by a "Planter" suggested that the planters force merchants into line by refusing to deal with any who continued to import British goods. Christopher Gadsden then offered a tentative draft of an appropriate non-importation agreement. Shortly thereafter the *Gazette* published another form of agreement, one that had been signed by most of the members of the Commons house. The following week, on July 4, the artisans met, amended, and signed this agreement. Meanwhile, the merchants attempted to build a backfire by adopting an agreement of their own, more to their liking. The problem then became one of reconciling the conflicting provisions of the various agreements, but on July 22, 1769, a large meeting approved a compromise. Neither slaves nor most manufactured British products were to be imported; the chief exceptions were such necessary items as firearms, hardware, and cheap cloth. Sanctions to insure compliance included a commercial boycott of all individuals who failed to sign within the month; those who reneged upon the agreement after signing were to merit "the utmost Contempt." Finally, a committee composed of thirteen merchants, thirteen artisans, and thirteen planters was to oversee enforcement of these provisions.

The initial wave of enthusiasm, augmented by gentle coercion, was sufficient to induce most persons to cooperate. Within a few weeks a correspondent assured readers of the *South-Carolina Gazette* that in addition to royal officials only thirty-one persons in town had failed to sign the agreement and that most of them were "*little* Scotch *Shop-keepers* of no consequence." Even one important royal official signed. To Lieutenant Governor Bull's intense annoyance, Robert

Raper subscribed and actually helped to foment "the popular discontents." Raper, who was the royal naval officer for
the port of Charleston, also served as the attorney for a local
estate. He, Bull reported, "judiciously and casuistically" dis-
tinguished between the two roles. Raper, the agent, signed;
Raper, the naval officer, did not.

At the other extreme, some equally important men refused to cooperate. John Gordon, a leading importer of goods
for the Indian trade, signed the original merchants' agreement. Then put under pressure to sign revised forms, he lost
patience and refused, as he put it, to "be bandyed about from
Resolutions to Resolutions." The confrontation between the
committee and two planters, William Wragg and William
Henry Drayton, was more dramatic. Wragg was a fiercely
independent individual who later became a loyalist; Drayton was a flamboyant political fledgling. Neither would
stand for having his personal freedom circumscribed by an
extralegal combination of men. The result of the attempt to
coerce them was a display of verbal pyrotechnics as each
side traded insults with the other in the local newspapers.
Wragg remained in South Carolina, but Drayton eventually
retreated to London where under the title of *The Letters of
Freeman* he published most of the essays written on both
sides of the controversy. A position on the Council rewarded
his efforts and he returned to assume his seat in April 1772,
only to switch sides as the pre-Revolutionary controversy
grew more intense.

As long as the majority signed or cooperated, an occa-
sional maverick like Wragg or Drayton represented only a
minor threat to the success of the embargo. But as the restrictions began to pinch merchants who had signed and hitherto
cooperated, the problem of enforcement became more seri-

ous. As a result, the committee attempted to keep backsliders in line by the threat of economic reprisal and violence. But it carefully selected the individuals with whom it clashed. One or two failures in challenging men of prestige and power might well have destroyed the non-importation movement, and the committee wisely considered that a leaky embargo was better than no embargo at all.

Consequently, non-importation worked reasonably well. Imports from Great Britain dropped by more than fifty percent, making this one of the most effective embargoes on the continent. At the time, South Carolinians estimated that non-importation saved them more than three hundred thousand pounds in payments to Great Britain. Impressive as these figures were, the immediate results were disappointing. Unlike the period of the Stamp Act crisis, the British economy was doing well, and trade with the rest of the world was able to take up much of the slack produced by the American embargo. Nevertheless, British merchants did request repeal of the Townshend duties and Lord North, who had taken Townshend's place at the exchequer, was eventually able to persuade his colleagues to make concessions. But once again, when actual repeal followed in April 1770, the willingness of British authorities to back down did not signify that they recognized the legitimacy of the colonial position. North urged repeal of the duties not because he believed them unconstitutional but because he was willing to concede that they had failed to carry out the government's overall policy of promoting British trade. To maintain the right to levy such taxes he retained the duty on tea.

The question for most Americans then became whether to continue non-importation until that duty was repealed as

well. For South Carolinians the question was different. They
had been nearly the last to institute non-importation, but
when they did so they demanded not only repeal of the
Townshend duties but also, in effect, reversal of the recent
trend of British policy toward the colonies. Thus the crucial
question for them was what to do when other Americans,
thinking their goal largely achieved and ignoring the tax on
tea, began to abandon non-importation. At first, South Carolinians resolved to have as few commercial dealings as possible with backsliders. But unity was obviously necessary to
the success of the movement, and particularly after New
York gave up in July 1770 non-importation collapsed
throughout most of the colonies. John MacKenzie, one of
the chief proponents of the boycott, published a slashing
attack on such perfidious conduct, but persistence increasingly appeared to be a futile gesture. And on December 13,
1770, Henry Laurens presided over a meeting which voted
to discontinue the embargo on all but tea.

Perhaps the most important result of the crisis over the
Townshend duties was the realization by many South Carolinians that arguments based on reason were going to change
few minds in London. As MacKenzie put it, "it is not the
head, but the heart that wants to be set aright." If imperial
authorities willfully refused to see the colonial point of view,
Americans could depend only upon themselves for redress
of their grievances. They would have to force Englishmen
to respect their rights. For the moment the means of coercion
was economic; the next time it might be arms. Although
they did not fully realize it yet, South Carolinians were hur-
rying down the road to rebellion. And they would arrive all
the more quickly because, unlike most other Americans, they
did not enjoy a quiet period between 1770 and 1773.

Chapter VI

The Wilkes Fund Controversy

"Scenes of a very extraordinary nature have opened on our legislative theater."

—Lieutenant Governor William Bull, Jr. (1773)

The uproar in the colonies over the Townshend duties coincided with one phase of the uproar in London over John Wilkes, a demogogic Englishman who had bedeviled ministries since the early 1760's. In February 1768, he returned from France where he had fled to escape a charge of seditious libel for having publicly called the king a liar. Though elected to Parliament by the voters of Middlesex County he was sent to prison instead where he seemed symbolically to represent all throughout the empire who felt themselves aggrieved by an "oppressive" ministry. "Wilkes and Liberty" became the toast of American gentlemen as well as the cry of the London mob. The Society of Gentlemen Supporters of the Bill of Rights, a group formed in London to offer Wilkes political and financial support, therefore solicited funds from Americans as well as Englishmen. One to whom they addressed a request was Christopher Gadsden; he in turn referred the matter to the Commons. And on December 8, 1769, the house ordered the treasurer, Jacob Motte, to send fifteen hundred pounds sterling to the society.

Whatever else can be said about this action, it was rash. Harassed at home and abroad, imperial authorities were

sure to be outraged at the insult. That many members of the
Commons later had reservations about what they had done
suggests that they did not fully consider the consequences
of their behavior. Hitherto other colonies had taken the lead
in resisting the Sugar Act, the Stamp Act, and the Townshend
duties. Here seemed to be a way for South Carolinians to
take the initiative in a manner which seemed to be particularly in character. Proud of their reputation for public
largess, they had already sought to justify it by erecting the
statue of William Pitt at public expense. The grant to Wilkes
was an action similar in kind, though different in degree.
How different may have escaped many persons in the enthusiasm of the moment.

What made the gift even more heinous in the eyes of the
ministry was the fact that the house had ordered the money
out of the treasury without the concurrence of the governor
and Council, who would of course have blocked it. But imperial authorities had long instructed the royal governor not
to permit disbursements which he and the Council had not
approved. In the past, however, the Commons alone had
occasionally met unusual expenses by borrowing from the
surplus in the treasury and then providing for repayment of
the sum in the annual tax bill. But never had the attention
of the ministry been so rudely called to the practice.

News of the grant therefore produced a violent reaction
in London. The matter was immediately referred to the
attorney general who reported that the practice of issuing
money from the treasury on the sole authority of the Commons was entirely unwarranted. Imperial authorities therefore decided to put a stop to the procedure, and on April 14,
1770, Secretary of State Hillsborough transmitted a new instruction to Bull. Under threat of being removed from office,

the governor was not to approve any revenue bill that did not contain specified restrictions on the expenditure of all money to be raised by the act. Moreover, all revenue measures were to include provisions inflicting severe penalties upon the colonial treasurer if he executed any order of the house not having the concurrence of the governor and Council.

If the house blundered in making the original grant, the ministry blundered in framing an instruction which no Commons could accept. It deprived the house of its power to issue public monies upon its own authority; it stipulated certain provisions to be incorporated in all future revenue bills, thereby seriously compromising the autonomous role of the Commons in originating and formulating money bills; and, as interpreted by the Council as well as by imperial authorities, it barred repayment of the sum already borrowed for the gift to Wilkes.

At first, the Commons believed that Bull or someone else had erroneously informed imperial officials that the house had recently assumed the power to order money from the treasury. The Commons therefore directed Garth to make clear to the ministry that ample precedent for the procedure existed. The ministry was unimpressed. Attorney General William De Grey had succinctly phrased their position when first reporting on the grant: ordering money from the treasury without the approval of governor and Council violated the intent of the governor's instructions and commission; it was therefore not "warranted by the modern practice of a few years, irregularly introduced, and improvidently acquiesced in." The ministry was adamant; if the impasse were to be resolved, the Commons would have to surrender this power.

Conversely, the house had no intention of compromising the other fundamental point at issue, its right to formulate money bills as it, and it alone, wished. Henry Laurens summed up the prevailing feeling: At stake was "nothing less than the very Essence of true Liberty," the *"Right* of the People to give and grant voluntarily in mode and in Quantity free from the Fetters of ministerial Instructions."

Gradually as the deadlock lengthened into years and each side began to comprehend the tenacity of the other the ingredients of a compromise seemed to be developing. Realizing that they had probably gone too far, many members of the Commons may have been willing to give up the power to issue money on their sole authority. Equally anxious to settle the controversy, imperial authorities indicated that they would accept the Commons' contention in regard to money bills and drop the relevant part of the instruction if the house would pass a declaratory act prohibiting it from issuing funds without the concurrence of governor and Council.

Nevertheless, a compromise failed to materialize, largely because of what might have been the least fundamental of the three issues raised by the instruction of April 1770. But repayment of the funds borrowed from the treasury to make the gift to Wilkes soon became the emotional focal point of the dispute. Royal authorities were determined to make the Commons repudiate the grant by preventing its repayment in a future tax bill. The Commons was equally determined not to repudiate it. By demanding that the house void a transaction to which it had already committed itself the ministry's efforts to stipulate what the tax bill should not contain posed the most provocative possible challenge to the power of the house in money matters.

Moreover, the issue was bound to be perennial; each time the legislature attempted to pass a tax bill, there it was to block the proceedings. The result was continual friction with the governor and councillors who felt obligated to support their superiors.

At first, the dispute with Governor Montagu was the most serious. Although he had been out of the colony much of the time since assuming his position in 1766, he was no longer a novice. Accordingly, he might have been expected to exhibit seasoned judgment. He did not. A rumor persists that after the Revolution began Montagu offered to fight for the Americans. Though implausible, the tale is consistent with his mecurial character. Immature and unstable, he prompted Speaker of the House Peter Manigault to remark that, although he liked to have a weak governor, Montagu convinced him that "it was not impossible for a Man to be too great a Fool to make a good Governor." Returning to South Carolina in September 1771, Montagu soon clashed with the Commons. Two treasurers, Benjamin Dart and Henry Peronneau, now filled the position vacated by Motte's death. Both refused to disburse money from the treasury without the concurrence of the governor and Council, whereupon the Commons ordered them committed to jail for contempt of its authority. Montagu rescued them by dissolving the house on November 5. When the new Commons met the following April, it refused to conduct any other business until permitted to pass a tax bill of its own devising. It was in session only a week before Montagu impatiently dissolved it. The governor then conceived a dangerously bright idea.

Why not move the assembly from Charleston to Beaufort, a small town on the coast some fifty miles further south?

In an attempt to remove the Massachusetts General Assembly from the influence of Boston, Secretary of State Hillsborough had recently instructed Governor Hutchinson to move it to Cambridge. The dispute that followed should have warned Montagu not to attempt a similar experiment. But he hoped that by meeting the assembly in an inconvenient location, he could induce the leaders of his opposition to remain at home in Charleston.

The result was a disaster. One newspaper essay noted that "No measure of any Governor was ever more freely and generally condemned." When the newly elected members set out for Beaufort they found that Montagu kept them waiting for three days—only to send them back to Charleston. Unknown to them, his behavior was the result of a disturbing letter which he had just received. Hillsborough, who was now trying to be more conciliatory, had written to Montagu directing him to have the house proceed to normal business as rapidly as possible. Montagu therefore found himself far out on an embarrassing limb at Beaufort. The return to Charleston was his attempt to retreat from a blunder from which there was now no escape.

Thereafter, the more he struggled to extricate himself, the deeper he sank. Upon reconvening in Charleston, the Commons appointed a committee on grievances which recommended a series of resolutions charging Montagu with "an Unwarrantable Abuse of a Royal Prerogative." The committee also recommended that Garth be directed to attempt to have the governor reprimanded or removed from his position. Expecting action of this kind, Montagu tried to protect himself by looking over the journals of the house each evening. When he sent for them the night after the committee made its report, the clerk informed him that the speaker of the house, Rawlins Lowndes, had taken them home, and Montagu did not receive the journals until the following morning. Finding the committee's recommendations, he sent for the Commons to cut off further proceedings by proroguing it. But before obeying the summons, the house debated and approved the committee's recommendations. Then, after the session ended, the committee of correspondence directed Garth to secure Montagu's removal. Montagu, enraged and thoroughly frightened, countered by dissolving that house and calling for new elections, which merely returned most of the old members, who promptly reelected Lowndes as speaker. Montagu ordered them to make another choice. They unanimously refused and he prorogued them. But in the process he made a minor procedural error which he feared might expose him to further censure. Having lost his perspective on the matter, he again attempted to protect himself by dissolving the house. It was the fourth dissolution in fifteen months. At this point Montagu retreated to England. Aware that imperial authorities were thoroughly disgusted with him, he soon resigned.

The chief stumbling block to normal business then proved to be the Council. Even before knowing of the ministry's instruction of April 1770, the councillors refused to countenance repayment of the Wilkes grant, which they considered neither "fit, or decent." The Commons countered by attempting to bar the Council from any role in the legislative process, contending that it was absurd for a Council composed mostly of royal officials to claim to be an upper house of the legislature. In reality, it was dependent upon

the executive and should therefore be considered nothing
but the governor's advisory body. This argument, which
dated back at least to the 1740's, became increasingly frequent and plausible in the 1760's as the Crown appointed
more placemen in the hope of insuring a pliant Council.

Early in August 1773 the upper house investigated the
state of the treasury and published a report which indicated
that the colony was nearly insolvent. Although the report
was exaggerated, there was some foundation for it. Due to
the continuing dispute no tax bill had been passed since
1769. Moreover, one of the unofficial perquisites of the
treasurer's office was the interest which could be collected
by lending public money at private profit. The Council's
investigation therefore discovered a large sum outstanding.
Most of it represented money owed to the treasury by local
merchants for goods imported subject to provincial duties.
Actually, the treasurers were legally responsible for these
funds. Nevertheless, the Council requested that Bull order
the attorney general to sue the merchants for the amount
due. Furthermore, the Council published its proceedings
regarding the matter in the local newspapers. By alarming
the public the Council clearly hoped to put pressure on the
Commons to pass a tax act. Disgusted, Bull refused to com-
ply with the Council's request which, he believed would
bring general distress and a "shock to Trade." The action
of the upper house seemed patently irresponsible.

Two could play this game, however, and the Commons
stood a considerably better chance of winning. The general
duty act, which would expire at the end of the current
legislative session, provided funds to pay Anglican clergy-
men and some civil officials. By not renewing the act, Bull

reported, the Commons hoped that pity might "flow from another Fountain"—that the Crown might give up its demands in order to protect members of the religious and civil establishment. To counter this strategy most of the councillors resolved to pass no legislation whatsoever until the Commons revived the general duty act. But the two Drayton's — John and William Henry, father and son — believed that their colleagues were unwarranted in attempting to dictate what the entire legislature could and could not pass. Consequently, they registered a formal protest.

On August 31, 1773, that protest appeared in the *South-Carolina Gazette,* currently printed by Thomas Powell. The Council promptly hauled him before it; demanded an explanation and an apology for "a high Breach of Privilege and a Contempt of this House"; and when one it deemed sufficient was not forthcoming, ordered him to jail. William Henry Drayton, who had been responsible for transmitting the protest to Powell in the first place, maintained that the whole purpose of a protest was vitiated unless its existence was public knowledge and that his own role in the matter absolved Powell from blame. The two Draytons therefore again formally protested the Council's action.

The man most responsible for Powell's commitment appears to have been the president of the Council, Sir Egerton Leigh, who had just returned from England in proud possession of a baronetcy and a firm resolution to uphold the authority of the Council. The British House of Lords, the House of Commons, and the local Commons House of Assembly each possessed the power to punish for contempt of its authority. Jailing Powell, Leigh undoubtedly reasoned, would therefore help to establish the validity of the Council's claim to the status of an upper house.

But in committing Powell to jail, Leigh and his colleagues made a serious mistake. Powell immediately applied for a writ of habeas corpus before two justices of the peace, Rawlins Lowndes, who was speaker of the House, and George Gabriel Powell, also a member of the Commons. Young Edward Rutledge, the attorney who represented the printer, rehearsed the increasingly familiar argument designed to prove that the Council was not an upper house of the legislature. Not being an upper house, it lacked the power to jail persons for the contempt of its authority. Therefore Powell should be released. Easily convinced, the two justices set Powell free. The Council attempted to retaliate by proceeding against the two justices themselves. Whereupon the Commons examined the whole case and resolved that the actions of the Council were unprecedented, unconstitutional, and "a Dangerous Violation of the Liberty of the Subject." The Commons then requested that Lieutenant Governor Bull suspend those responsible for Powell's commitment. Orders followed to Garth directing him to obtain their permanent removal. Meanwhile, Thomas Powell sued Leigh for damages arising from his arrest. Chief Justice Thomas Knox Gordon—himself a member of the Council—now reversed the opinion of the two justices and dismissed the suit on the grounds that, being an upper house of the legislature, the Council exercised legitimate powers in arresting Powell. Yet many South Carolinians remained unimpressed by this judicial pronouncement. As a result, Leigh's attempt to strengthen the Council only further weakened it.

By defending the Council and castigating the Commons in a pamphlet entitled *Considerations on Certain Political Transactions of the Province of South Carolina,* published in London in January 1774, Leigh attempted to redeem matters. In reply Laurens and Ralph Izard induced the Virginian Arthur Lee to compose an *Answer to Considerations on Certain Political Transactions of the Province of South Carolina.* By this time, however, the Boston Tea Party had engrossed the attention of nearly everyone and neither pamphlet made much of a stir in London or South Carolina.

The time for argument had passed; the time for action had come—or so the Commons reasoned. By the spring of 1774 South Carolina was entering its fourth year of governmental paralysis and the fifth without a tax bill. In response to Indian turmoil on the frontier the house drafted a bill to raise and pay for a troop of rangers. Apparently the Commons hoped that the emergency would force the governor and Council to accept the bill without the stipulations directed by the instruction of April 1770, but the upper house remained adamant. The Commons then cut the Gordian knot. Auditing the accounts of debts due by the government as in preparing a regular tax bill, the house without the concurrence of the governor and Council issued certificates in payment of the outstanding accounts. Signed by the clerk and five of the most important representatives, these certificates were redeemable for regular currency as soon as a tax bill could be passed. In the meantime, the members of the house and of the Charleston Chamber of Commerce promised to accept this paper at face value. The Council protested, and Bull prorogued the legislature in reprisal, but except for Bull everyone (including the councillors) accepted the certificates in lieu of money. Thereafter passage of a tax bill was not an immediately pressing problem. Moreover, the controversy soon became submerged in the turmoil following the Boston Tea Party.

Nevertheless the dispute over the donation to Wilkes was immensely important, perhaps most of all because it revealed, more clearly than any previous controversy, a fundamental point at issue between imperial authorities and local leaders. Leigh voiced the opinion of the former when he wrote that the constitution of the colony was completely *"derivative"* from the Crown. In other words, the rights and privileges of the Commons were solely those which the Crown permitted it to have. Thus, no matter how many precedents the house might be able to cite to justify the exercise of rights, privileges, and powers acquired over the years, these could be wiped out by royal fiat. Arthur Lee spoke for South Carolina's leaders: "The Rights and Privileges of the Commons House spring from the Rights and Privileges of British Subjects, and are coeval with the Constitution. They were neither created, nor can they be abolished by the Crown." Furthermore, "what has prevailed from the Beginning of the Colony, without Question or Controul, is Part of the Constitution." That is, local practice and precedent were integral parts of the colonial constitution which ought to be respected by imperial authorities. But what if they did not? As the unilateral action of the Commons in issuing certificates to pay public creditors demonstrated, many South Carolinians were increasingly ready to give a vigorous reply.

Chapter VII

The Tea Act Crisis

"Upon the same Principle all in Charles-Town might be laid in Ashes."
—"A Carolinian" (1774)

Because of the dispute over the Wilkes fund, intense political conflict disrupted the regular functioning of government during the last six years of the colonial period. Partly because of the controversy over the tax on tea, a new government evolved to replace the old. For South Carolinians, as well as other Americans, the Boston Tea Party was a final turning point in the road to Revolution.

Seeking to rescue the East India Company from dire financial straits, the British government permitted it to ship tea directly to the American colonies, thereby eliminating the costs of British duties and middlemen. Although the measure meant that Americans would be able to buy English tea at a lower price than before—in fact, more cheaply than smuggled tea—many of them failed to appreciate their new advantages. Merchants involved in the tea trade were concerned about competition from consignees of the East India Company. More importantly, most Americans had long since become suspicious of imperial authorities bearing gifts, and they saw an ulterior purpose in the apparent concession. The arrangement, they concluded, was designed to induce them to buy the company's tea and thereby give de facto recognition to the legitimacy of the tea duty. They

51

were partly right; had the aim been merely to relieve the East India Company, the duty paid in America might have been removed rather than duties paid in England. Being realists, many patriot leaders concluded that the only way to prevent most Americans from buying the cheaper dutied tea was to deliver them from temptation.

Throughout the colonies men made plans to send the tea back to England without allowing it to be landed. In some ports, such as Philadelphia, the plan worked; in others, such as Charleston and Boston, it did not. On December 1, 1773, the *London,* with 257 chests of tea aboard, arrived in the harbor at Charleston. Two days later at the Exchange building a mass meeting revitalized the moribund non-importation agreement against tea, and the consignees of the East India Company resigned their commissions. But within the next three weeks the tea would become legally liable to seizure for nonpayment of duties. How to prevent its being seized, landed, and later sold, therefore, became a more urgent question as time went on. Fortunately, South Carolinians debated too long. And early on December 22, Lieutenant Governor Bull and the customs officers unloaded the tea and stored it under the Exchange, where it remained until sold during the Revolution to help finance the patriot war effort. Events were more violent in Boston, where on December 16 well-organized crews boarded the tea ships and heaved about 342 chests of the East India Company's tea overboard.

The reaction was primarily one of shock in the colonies and outrage in London. After all, the tea was the private property of the company, and the sacredness of private property had been one of the chief American concerns throughout the long dispute with imperial authorities. Many Americans thought the Bostonians had clearly gone too far. The British ministry, quite understandably, decided that stringent measures were in order. Parliament passed a law closing the port of Boston until the East India Company and the customs service were compensated for the lost tea and duties. Later in the spring, the Administration of Justice Act authorized trials in England for royal officers accused of capital crimes committed while on duty in America. In addition, the Massachusetts Government Act, passed the same day, drastically modified the Massachusetts charter of 1691.

The Intolerable Acts, as Americans termed them, were designed to divide and cow Americans by making an example of Massachusetts. The result was exactly the opposite. Upon hearing of these acts, most South Carolinians forgot their previous horror at the violence of the tea party. Outrage and concern over what they considered to be tyrannical measures followed. To their overwrought imaginations, the Administration of Justice Act seemed to declare an open hunting season on Americans; the "Murder Act," they called it. By preventing the use of all wharves and vessels the Boston Port Act appeared to confiscate the property of every merchant in Boston, innocent and guilty alike. By the same reasoning, one newspaper propagandist argued, "if a few ill-minded Persons were to take upon them to make Water against the Door of a Customs-house Officer . . . All in Charles-Town might be laid in Ashes." Somewhat less graphically, Laurens saw the Coercive Acts as precedents for laws to "Cram down . . . every Mandate which Ministers Shall think proper for keeping us in Subjection to the Task

Master who Shall be put over us." Fear of what next lay
in store for them made South Carolinians ready and willing
to aid Boston.

The question was how. The Boston town meeting asked
for another general boycott of British goods; inhabitants
of New York City wished to defer non-importation until
the colonies could concert measures in another meeting
similar to the Stamp Act Congress. Massachusetts eventually
agreed and on June 17, 1774, the House of Representatives
called for a general colonial congress to be held in Philadelphia the following September.

Meanwhile South Carolinians had begun to establish
extra-legal machinery to enforce the boycott on tea. A mass
meeting on January 20 appointed a large steering committee
to prepare for future mass meetings. News of the Boston
Port Act brought another meeting which authorized the
general committee to call elections for representatives to a
gathering on July 6. When they met, 104 delegates chosen
from nearly every part of the colony joined everyone in
Charleston who wished to attend "the most general meeting
that has ever been known." The description is that of Edward Rutledge who also reported that "almost every man
of consequence" attended.

Business took three days. After adopting resolutions con-
demning the most recent British measures, the meeting
considered the calls to participate in a non-importation
movement and a continental congress. There was wide support for the latter, but no decision could be reached about
non-importation. The group did, however, vote to give its
delegates to the congress power to agree to joint measures.
The composition of the delegation therefore became the

important question. Remembering their difficulties during earlier crises, merchants responded to harbingers of trouble over tea by organizing the Charleston Chamber of Commerce. Spurred by the new organization, they mobilized the votes of their clerks; artisans and others countered by canvassing the town in behalf of their own candidates. The result was the choice of Henry Middleton, John and Edward Rutledge, Christopher Gadsden, and Thomas Lynch. (Instead of the latter three, the merchants would have preferred Miles Brewton, Charles Pinckney, and Rawlins Lowndes.) Before adjourning, the meeting elected a committee of ninety-nine, consisting of fifteen merchants, fifteen mechanics, and sixty-nine planters, one of whom—Charles Pinckney — became chairman. Empowered to act as the executive agent of the general meeting, this committee virtually became the temporary government of South Carolina.

Meeting from September 5 to October 26, 1774, the First Continental Congress took important steps. By an extremely close vote it rejected Joseph Galloway's "Plan of a Proposed Union between Great Britain and the Colonies" which would have established an American legislature to have concurrent jurisdiction with Parliament over colonial affairs. Declarations and resolves enumerating American rights and denouncing recent British measures followed. Congress also adopted a "Continental Association" pledging Americans to embargo most trade with Great Britain. Committees to enforce this association were to be elected in every city, town, and county throughout America. Before adjourning, Congress then explained its stand in formal addresses to the king and to the people of Great Britain and America.

It also resolved to meet again on May 10, 1775, unless American grievances were redressed in the meantime.

Throughout the meeting Gadsden and Lynch played especially conspicuous parts. Gadsden, impulsive and impassioned as ever, left "all New England Sons of Liberty far behind," one delegate from Connecticut noted. Since he apparently moved that a preventive attack be immediately launched against British forces in Boston, the estimate seems accurate. Thomas Lynch, who later reported from the Second Continental Congress that business "now goes on Swimmingly, for Why? my Colleague Gadsden is gone home, to Command our troops, God save them," was more stable. Invariably he impressed men as being a plain "man of sense" who "carries with him more force in his very appearance than most powdered folks in their conversation." Nevertheless, he was as deeply committed to the defense of American rights as Gadsden. On the opening day, Lynch made three successful motions which represented victories for those who favored vigorous measures: that Congress meet in Carpenters Hall, that Peyton Randolph preside, and that Charles Thomson be secretary.

But the most dramatic incident involving members of the South Carolina delegation developed over the question of non-exportation. On October 20, just when the Association appeared ready for signing, all of the South Carolinians except Gadsden walked out, demanding that the colony be permitted to continue exporting rice and indigo. Gadsden, as usual, was willing to make drastic sacrifices to obtain unified action. The others led by John Rutledge believed that unless the exemption was granted, South Carolina would be saddled with a disproportionately heavy burden. Neither the middle nor New England colonies were dependent upon enumerated products, but most rice and all indigo could be shipped only within the empire. The agreement, therefore, threatened to cut South Carolinians off from their major market. Eventually Rutledge and his colleagues proved willing to compromise. In return for permission to export rice, they agreed to accept an embargo on indigo. Rather than break up the Congress, delegates from other colonies approved this arrangement.

Chapter VIII

The Association and the Outbreak of Hostilities

"It would take many Sheets to contain and days to write the History of our proceedings. . . ."

—Henry Laurens (1775)

On November 6, the returning South Carolinians arrived in Charleston and the general committee promptly called elections for a provincial congress to meet on January 11, 1775. When this Congress met, trouble quickly developed over the terms of the Association. Because he considered the exemption of rice to be divisive, Gadsden recommended that South Carolinians now agree not to export rice. Rutledge argued that the exemption should be retained. His arguments were sound, but they also applied to indigo. Back-country planters grew indigo but not rice, and they naturally felt themselves to be the victims of an invidious distinction. To placate them a rather cumbersome plan was devised by which a third of the rice crop would be used to compensate those who produced other products. Committees to enforce the Association were established in each area. More ominously, the Provincial Congress also recommended that all inhabitants of the colony "be diligently attentive in learning the use of arms." And finally, the Provincial Congress reelected the same delegation to the Second Continental Congress.

Even before the provisions of the Association were known,

South Carolinians adopted similar measures on their own initiative. At first the chief effort appears to have been directed toward erecting the machinery of enforcement. Goods imported from Great Britain were confiscated and put up for sale at public auction. In theory, the proceeds were intended for the relief of suffering Bostonians. In practice, the contribution to that cause was largely made up of donations. There were no profits to send, because the process of confiscation and auction initially represented only a dress rehearsal. The owner of the goods was allowed to bid for them at their original cost; since this was re-funded to him, he kept his property at the price of only a little inconvenience.

On February 1 rigorous enforcement replaced early leniency. How rigid that enforcement could be soon became apparent. Robert Smythe, a Charleston merchant, returned from England late in March bringing with him personal property used in England. It included two English horses. Could they be landed? On the grounds that they repre-sented personal property previously acquired and not in-tended for sale, the Charleston committee decided that they could be. But the populace at large believed that this decision violated the terms of the Association. If implemented, they argued, it would destroy the entire non-importation move-ment—which it might have, once the notion that Smythe received special treatment became prevalent. The hubbub forced the committee to reconsider the matter and by a close vote to rescind its earlier decision. Lieutenant Governor Bull wryly observed that "the many headed power of the people" was not now so easily controlled by its former leaders. Inter-estingly enough, those leaders had gained an unexpected recruit, William Henry Drayton, who now demanded that the committee listen to the voice of the people.

Drayton's conversion from one of the loudest supporters of the prerogative to one of the most demagogic leaders of the Revolution is puzzling. He was clearly volatile and ambitious, and historians have sometimes ascribed his actions to resentment at having his personal and economic ambitions thwarted by royal officials. That he developed an intense dislike for placemen suggests that this interpretation may be at least partly correct. Furthermore, like many of the younger Revolutionary leaders in South Carolina, he had recently been to England. Perhaps an anonymous writer in the *Gazette* was not too wide of the mark in observing that "when any of our great men go over" to England they expect to be "as important upon the Royal Exchange as they have been under our Vendue House. A little experience shows them their mistake; and after having run out something more than their income in supporting their ideal importance, they find England to be a land of slaves, and betake themselves in high dudgeon to their native swamps." Perhaps all of these elements contributed to Drayton's change of heart, and none precludes a sincere change of mind about the locus of the threat to liberty. At any rate, like many converts, he became a zealous champion of the new cause.

His flair for publicity made each step in his progress from proto-loyalist to flaming revolutionary a step toward Revolution for South Carolina as well. After the Powell affair, he repeatedly clashed with his colleagues on the Council. Meanwhile, he composed another pamphlet addressed to the Continental Congress in which he advocated a plan for an American legislature resembling Joseph Galloway's. A judge, he made a memorable circuit in November 1774 on which he charged grand juries to maintain the constitution inviolate "even at the Hazard of your Lives and Fortunes." Most of the juries—including the one at Ninety-Six of which Alexander Cameron was foreman—responded by presenting as a dangerous grievance Parliament's attempt to tax America. Because Cameron was the deputy of John Stuart, the royal superintendent of Indian affairs, the action of the Ninety-Six jury was the source of great glee to American patriots. Embarrassed officials attempted to comfort themselves with the rumor that while deliberating their action the jury drank more than one hundred bottles of port wine. Drayton's activities soon produced a request from the placemen on the Council that he be removed from it. On March 1, 1775, Lieutenant Governor Bull complied and suspended his nephew. Six weeks later, Drayton headed the secret committee which descended upon the public powder magazines and armory to remove arms and ammunition. In response to Bull's inquiry the Commons reported that it was unable to discover the perpetrators of the crime but "there is reason to suppose that some of the Inhabitants of this Colony may have been induced to take so extraordinary and uncommon a step in consequence of the late alarming Accounts from Great Britain."

The news was indeed alarming. On February 27, 1775, the British House of Commons approved the ministry's plan for conciliating the American colonies. Parliament would "forebear" to tax any American colony that made adequate contributions toward paying for the common defense and civil government. As Americans immediately

realized, nothing in these provisions recognized the claim
to the exclusive right to tax themselves, and imperial officials remained judges of what constituted an adequate contribution. Moreover, the ministry also drafted a bill to
prohibit inhabitants of New England from trading outside
the empire and to bar them from their usual fishing grounds
in the North Atlantic. The bill became law on March 30;
two weeks later its provisions were extended to four more
colonies including South Carolina. By mid-April, South
Carolinians could not yet know the full cup of woe being
prepared for them, but early in May letters from London
reported that the British planned to incite Indian attacks
and slave rebellions in South Carolina. The report was
exaggerated but, given the heated atmosphere and the tra-
ditional fear of insurrection, it made a plausible rumor.
And almost immediately on top of this report came accounts
of the battles of Lexington and Concord.

The general committee therefore called the Provincial
Congress into session on June 1. Moving with great alacrity,
the Congress raised troops, authorized paper currency to pay
for them, and called for the election of a new Congress to
meet on December 1. It also established a council of safety
composed of thirteen members to act as an interim executive. And perhaps most indicative of the climate of opinion,
members of the Congress adopted and signed "an association," pledging to "UNITE ourselves, under every tie of
religion and of honor" to defend America and, if necessary,
"to sacrifice our lives and fortunes to secure her freedom
and safety." Henry Laurens, who had replaced Charles
Pinckney as president of the Congress, vigorously opposed
attempts to stigmatize men who would not sign the Associa-

tion. He was overruled. As a loyalist, Archibald Baird, discovered as early as six months before, it was "even culpable to be passive." Tar and feathers and similar measures came into fashion.

Despite the efforts of moderate men like Laurens, hysteria —and perhaps the need to rouse and unite the people—led to violence. When Lord William Campbell, the new royal governor, arrived on June 18 he found nearly everyone to be greatly excited by a rumor that he brought with him arms for slaves and Indians. Thus a free Negro, Thomas Jeremiah, was executed for supposedly inciting insurrection, though the evidence against him was flimsy. Campbell tried to intercede but was told that if he did not desist, he would be forced to hang Jeremiah at his own door. About three months earlier John Stuart had prudently fled southward, first to Savannah and then St. Augustine. Although he wished no general Indian war, he was not able to convince many South Carolinians of the sincerity of his statements. Other royal officials and intrepid loyalists were hauled before the general committee, disarmed, and confined to the city. William Wragg, the most important native South Carolinian among the group and long a thorn in the side of American patriots, courageously told the tribunal that he would abhor himself if he "was capable, upon any consideration, of subscribing to an opinion contrary to the dictates" of his own judgment. His outspokenness made him dangerous, particularly in Charleston. He was therefore ordered to be confined to his plantation near Dorchester. Meanwhile vessels sent out by the council of safety seized gunpowder from ships off the Georgia and Florida coasts. As the members of the Commons told Campbell during its

last session, "every Pacific Measure which human Wisdom
could devise has been used." Leaving "the justice of our
Cause to the Great Sovereign of the Universe, upon whom
the fate of Kingdoms and Empires depend," they prepared
for war.

More immediately, however, the fate of South Carolina
depended upon the unity of its people, and many men in
the back country were apathetic or actively hostile to the
measures being taken in Charleston. Historians have offered various explanations for this. Perhaps one of the
simplest is one of the best. Isolated and not yet really incorporated into the local government, many of these settlers
were recent immigrants into the colony. It was therefore
often easier for them to identify themselves as subjects of
the king than as citizens of South Carolina. Moreover, to
all but unusually well-educated men many of the pre-Revolutionary disputes, especially those involving the rights of
the Commons, must have seemed irrelevant and unimpor-
tant.

Whatever the reasons for their loyalty to the Crown,
many back-country men soon showed that they could not be
counted on to support the Revolution. On July 12, 1775,
Whigs obeyed the order of the council of safety to seize the
arms and ammunition at Fort Charlotte located on the
Savannah River some thirty miles southwest of the settle-
ment at Ninety-Six. Major James Mayson (who was in
charge of the operation) then moved a portion of the stores
to Ninety-Six. But Moses Kirkland, a thorough-going op-
portunist who had helped to take the ammunition, suspected
that a majority in the back country was unhappy about the
trend of events in Charleston. He therefore sent an emissary

to Colonel Thomas Fletchall of the Upper Saluda Militia Regiment to suggest that Fletchall recapture the powder on behalf of the Crown. Though sympathetic to the idea, Fletchall was not a decisive man. He therefore refused to take an active part in the scheme. His immediate subordinates were men of more resolution. Leading two hundred militia, they retook the ammunition and arrested Mayson for having stolen it.

Alarmed at events in the back country and perhaps hoping temporarily to rid itself of the influence of two firebrands, the council of safety requested that William Henry Drayton and the Reverend William Tennent go to the back country and attempt to convince its inhabitants of the justice of the American position. Because many of them were dissenters, Tennent was a particularly good choice. Pastor of the Congregational church in Charleston, he was—like Drayton —an ardent supporter of American rights and a superb propagandist. Joined by Oliver Hart, a Baptist Minister from Charleston, the men tackled the task with amazing energy. After a long, hot day in August which ended in a ride through pouring rain, Tennent noted in his diary, "if we can stand this we need fear nothing"—to which he added, but the storm "was not to be compared to the fury of the little Inhabitants of the Bed. After a sleepless and wet Night I was shocked by the Blood and Slaughter of my Callicoed Shirt and Sheets in the morning." But, despite these and greater sacrifices, the mission was not a complete success. Meeting effective opposition from Thomas Brown, one of the ablest and most persistent champions of the Crown in the back country, and others, Drayton concluded that the council of safety should arrest its leading opponents.

He therefore established headquarters at Ninety-Six and
sent out parties to capture suspected individuals. In turn,
the Tories raised a large number of men. Drayton then
prudently offered to negotiate with Fletchall who had now
taken over command of the loyalist force. Meanwhile, Drayton issued calls for help to trustworthy militia. By the
second week in September Fletchall and Drayton, each with
about one thousand men, faced each other across the Saluda
River. Negotiations followed. And on September 16, 1775,
Fletchall over the objections of his chief subordinates
agreed to a treaty of neutrality. Drayton then headed back
to the Congarees where on September 25 he conferred with
a number of Cherokee chiefs who were upset because few
trading goods had lately reached them. Drayton explained
why and promised to send them as much as could be spared.

Meanwhile a loyalist, Patrick Cunningham, raised a number of men to rescue his brother Robert who had been
jailed on charges of sedition. On November 3, he captured a
wagon train carrying gunpowder to the Cherokees. Claim-
ing that the Provincial Congress intended the ammunition
for a general Indian raid on the frontier, the loyalists re-
cruited a force that soon outnumbered that of Andrew
Williamson, a Whig major, who had called out his men at
news of the capture. Williamson therefore retreated from
Long Canes to Ninety-Six. On November 19 Major Joseph
Robinson led a group of Tories against him. The battle
which ensued lasted for three days and drew blood on both
sides, the first blood of the Revolution in South Carolina.
On the 22nd both sides were ready for a truce—Williamson's because they had only two cartridges per man left
and, for most of the time, no water except what they could

scoop out of hog troughs; Robinson's because they wished to escape before Whig reinforcements arrived.

Having received word of Cunningham's capture of the powder train, the Provincial Congress directed Colonel Richard Richardson of the Camden militia to call up his men, recapture the powder, and seize those who had taken it. The truce arranged by Robinson and Williamson did not, Richardson believed, apply to his own forces which soon numbered nearly twenty-five hundred men, including units from North Carolina. By December 12 he had captured Fletchall and many other leading loyalists.

Adding men as he went, Richardson's formidable force moved southwest from the Enoree River toward Ninety-Six. Badly outnumbered but uncowed, about 130 of the loyalists fled into the Cherokee country, established a camp on the Reedy River, and tried without success to rouse the Cherokees in their behalf. Here Richardson's expeditionary force surprised them, killed a number, and captured most of the rest, who were later released by the council of safety. As Richardson's army turned back it began to snow, and from then until they were disbanded on January 1, 1776, the men, unprepared for bad weather, suffered in two weeks of snow, sleet, and rain. Nevertheless, the "snow campaign" was a great success. Not until the British capture of Charleston were the Tories again to be a serious problem in the back country.

Meanwhile equally important developments were occurring in Charleston. Suspecting that Governor Campbell maintained communications with the loyalists, a Whig, who claimed to be one of the king's friends, visited him. Campbell fell into the trap. The next day he quietly moved his powerless office from Charleston to a British vessel in the harbor. Thus on September 15, 1775, the last vestige of royal government finally collapsed.

The Second Provincial Congress took its place. Elected in the fall, its members assembled on November 1 and remained in session until the 29th. William Henry Drayton, who had just returned from the back country, was chosen as president—perhaps in an attempt to silence him. If so, it was unsuccessful. Congress also appointed a new council of safety which included most of the old members. In addition, Congress directed that some of the channels into the harbor be blocked. When a vessel attempting to execute this order drew fire from the *Tamar,* a British sloop of war, on November 11, war came to Charleston.

Chapter IX

The New State Sustained Against Her Enemies

"The Almighty Created America to be independent of Britain."
     —William Henry Drayton (1776)

A week before this encounter the Continental Congress advised South Carolinians to "establish such form of Government as in their judgment will best produce the happiness of the people, and most effectually secure peace and good order" during the dispute with Great Britain. Establishing such a government was the work of the Provincial Congress in the session lasting from February 1 to March 26, 1776. A committee composed of such influential men as John Rutledge, Christopher Gadsden, and Henry Laurens was promptly appointed to formulate plans for a temporary government. At times it appears that they turned for guidance to John Adams' *Thoughts on Government*, recently composed for just such occasions. More often they turned to colonial experience. In fact, the very idea of a written constitution evolved, at least in part, from the colonial charters and governors' instructions. Moreover, like the British constitution which developed partly through legislative enactment, the new state constitution would be merely an act of the legislature—though everyone agreed that one of the most important functions of a constitution was to limit the power of government. Here was the anomaly which eventually led to the idea of a constitutional convention.

69

South Carolina, however, was the first colony in the South
and only the second in the nation to draft a new state constitution. At this stage it was not unusual to utilize legislatures for the purpose.

More unusual were some of the provisions of the new
constitution. Unlike most of the first American governors,
John Rutledge possessed a veto over legislation. Furthermore, he was eligible for reelection. Undoubtedly, political
considerations and the relative scarcity of qualified men to
fill positions influenced these provisions. But it is equally
probable that the confidence South Carolinians developed
in their political leaders during the late colonial period
prompted them to trust these men with unusually wide
powers. Years of contending that the royal Council was not
an upper house bore fruit in provisions separating the
privy council, the governor's advisory body, from the
legislative council, the upper house of the assembly. Similarly, judges acquired tenure in their offices during good
behavior, and the lower house received a clear acknowledg-
ment of its exclusive right to draft money bills. The back
country, which contained more than 50 percent of the
population, was allocated approximately one-third of the
seats in the general assembly. The proportion was considerably larger than it possessed under royal government but
less than what present notions of one man one vote would
call for. All in all, the constitution of 1776 substantiated
the claim made by the First Provincial Congress that "no
love of innovation—no desire of altering the constitution
of government—no lust of independence has had the least
influence upon our Counsels." Undoubtedly upon settle-
ment of the disputes with Great Britain most individuals

hoped to retain the reforms contained in the constitution of 1776. Beyond this, very few wished to go. Almost everyone considered the goal to be acceptable terms of reconciliation with Britain, not independence.

Yet, as British authorities proved to be intransigent, the logic of the situation seemed to make independence the only real alternative to capitulation. In February 1776 Gadsden arrived in Charleston from the Continental Congress bringing a superb piece of propaganda in behalf of separation from the empire, Thomas Paine's *Common Sense.* Henry Laurens and most of his colleagues in the Provincial Congress found it full of "indecent" expressions toward the Crown. Nevertheless, on March 23 they empowered their delegates in the Continental Congress to agree to whatever measures Congress thought necessary for the general welfare. When the time came, Edward Rutledge, Thomas Heyward, Jr., Thomas Lynch, Jr., and Arthur Middleton, with varying degrees of reluctance, would construe this authorization so as to permit them to sign the Declaration of Independence. Of the few men who seemed to welcome the drift toward independence, one of the most conspicuous was William Henry Drayton. Elected chief justice of the state, perhaps once again in an unsuccessful attempt to silence him, on April 23 he delivered a widely circulated charge to the Charleston grand jury in which he contrasted the advantages of the new constitution with the disadvantages of British rule. "The Almighty created America to be independent of Britain," he concluded. "Let us beware of the impiety of being backward to act as instruments in the Almighty hand, now extended to accomplish his purpose."

If Drayton's analysis was correct, among the Lord's instruments for making South Carolinians willing to accept independence was the British attack on Charleston at the end of June 1776. Planning for the expedition was long and involved, and by the time the British forces, commanded by Sir Henry Clinton and Sir Peter Parker, arrived off Charleston, delays, mismanagement, and bad luck had warped the original purpose beyond recognition. Thus what began as an attempt to rally and support loyalists, especially in North Carolina, ended as a demonstration against Charleston.

Aware that the city might be the focus of attack, South Carolinians prepared to defend it. Buildings along the Cooper River were leveled and cannon mounted to sweep the area. Men poured into the city, nearly four thousand South Carolinians—regulars and militia—and another two hundred continentals from North Carolina and Virginia. With them came Major General Charles Lee, a professional soldier, once with the British army, now with the American. Lee's presence was a tonic for the morale of South Carolinians, though he himself was unimpressed by their efforts. Two months later he wrote from Georgia, "the people here are if possible more harum skarum than [in] their sister colony [South Carolina]." They suggest, he continued, all kinds of schemes without considering their practicability. "I shou'd not be surpris'd if they were to propose mounting a body of Mermaids on Alligators." Lacking mermaids to oppose the British, South Carolinians relied on the garrison in two forts. Fort Johnson on James Island was a sturdy structure. Gadsden and the First South Carolina Infantry manned. it. About four miles to the east on Sullivan's Island, commanding the main channel, was an unfinished fort being constructed of palmetto logs. General Lee took one look and termed it a slaughter pen, but Governor Rutledge vetoed its abandonment. Colonel William Moultrie and the Second South Carolina Infantry had the unenviable job of manning this fort. At the northern end of Sullivan's Island Colonel William Thomson with a force of about eight hundred men protected Moultrie from an attack on the landward side.

On June 28 the battle took place. The British plan of attack called for Clinton's men, already ashore on what is now the Isle of Palms, to cross the small tidal creek between it and Sullivan's Island and to attack Moultrie in the rear. Three of Parker's frigates were to run past Fort Sullivan and take position to its southwest where they would be well out of the range of Fort Johnson's guns but still able to bring their own cannon to bear on the unfinished side of Fort Sullivan. Unfortunately for the British the creek at the north end of Sullivan's Island was too deep and the shoals at the south end were too shallow. Clinton's troops found crossing in the face of Thomson's men to be impossible. As a result, the navy was forced to attack without support from the army. Three of Parker's vessels then managed to pass the fort—only to run hard aground. Impotent sitting ducks, they took a terrific pounding from Moultrie's cannon, while the rest of the fleet was able to do little damage to the fort's spongy palmetto logs which absorbed shot like sand bags. By nightfall Moultrie had sustained less than forty casualties; Parker more than four times as many. One frigate which had run aground, the *Actaeon*, was destroyed to prevent capture; several other vessels were heavily damaged. "Thus," as one British army officer reported, were, "2 fifty Gunn Ships 5 frigates and a

Bomb of the Invincible British Navy defeated by a Battery which it was supposed would not have stood one Broadside." And, thus ended the first British attack on Charleston.

Shortly thereafter, full-scale Indian war broke out on the frontier. Williamson raised the militia as rapidly as he could and by the end of July had nearly twelve hundred men. Marching to attack the Cherokees, he was ambushed early on the morning of August 1 as his force crossed the Keowee River but pushed on to devastate the Indian settlements east of the Blue Ridge Mountains. Meanwhile General Griffith Rutherford and Colonel William Christian led North Carolinians and Virginians, respectively, in laying waste the more remote Indian towns. Thoroughly beaten, the Indians eventually agreed to a treaty ceding large areas of land to South Carolina, North Carolina, and Virginia.

The battle of Fort Moultrie and the fighting on the frontier made it easier for many South Carolinians to accept independence, but many others remained reluctant. At least for the low-country elite, mid-eighteenth-century South Carolina had been a very comfortable place, prosperous and well-governed. To exchange the known for the unknown, that which had proved capable of providing the good life for the opportunities and dangers of independence, hardly seemed an attractive prospect. Henry Laurens wept at the thought of independence, and he undoubtedly expressed the feelings of many of his friends when he wrote that he felt like a dutiful son driven "by the hand of violence" from his father's house. But though the ties of sentiment and economic interest helped to bind South Carolinians to the empire, other considerations prevailed.

"A Free British American" from Charleston posed the

crucial question, "Is the selfish Nature of Man so much mended, is his Lust for Power so far satiated, that we may resign ourselves, with unsuspecting Confidence, into the Hands of the Fox Hunters and Gamblers of St. Stephen's Chapel?" Neither the fox hunters of Parliament nor the ministry intended to establish despotic rule over the colonies. At first, they merely attempted to make Americans pay what Englishmen considered to be a fair share of the cost of defending and governing the empire. When that attempt elicited a challenge to the power of Parliament, they resolved, above all, to uphold the sovereignty of Parliament over the entire empire. For to them, it seemed that to compromise the one was to shatter the other. Yet South Carolinians, as well as other Americans, believed just as firmly that, human nature being what it was, to resign themselves into the hands of Parliament would be the utmost folly. To protect themselves they therefore turned to their own Commons House of Assembly, over which they had the requisite controls, and tried to mark out for it the widest possible area free from the interference of outside authorities. In particular, they attempted to insure that it possessed exclusive jurisdiction over the crucial area of public finance. To support their claims they invoked two constitutions, the provincial and the imperial. Tennyson later spoke of England, the land "where Freedom slowly broadens down from precedent to precedent." South Carolinians, believing that they shared all the rights of Englishmen, attributed a similar quality of organic growth to their own provincial constitution. They found that imperial authorities disagreed. Similarly, South Carolinians eventually contended that the only link between themselves and their fellow subjects in Great Britain was the king, that their own Commons was a small equivalent of the British House of Commons, to which they were not subject. This, too, they found to be an unacceptable argument in London. Ultimately, therefore, they came to the reluctant conclusion that William Henry Drayton was right, that "Americans can have no safety but by the Divine favor, their own virtue, and their being so prudent as *not to leave it in the power of the British rulers to injure them.*"

Here in the notion that, given the power, British rulers— or any man—might injure them, was the nexus of public-spirit and self-interest, private right and public right, principle and emotion. Ambition, resentment, frustration, anger— but most of all—the sad knowledge of human beings drove loyal South Carolinians out of the empire.

Yet if most went in sorrow, some went in hope. "When the mere Politician weighs the Danger or Safety of his Country," William Tennent said, "he computes them in Proportion to its Fortresses, Arms, Money, Provisions, Numbers of Fighting Men, and its Enemies; but when the Christian Patriot weighs the Danger and Safety of his Country, he computes them by its Numbers of sinful or praying People, and its Degrees of Holiness and Vice." Implicit in these words was the hope that the Revolution would lead to a moral renovation of American society. Other men, some with noble and some with ignoble goals, would also see in the Revolution the possibility of a new and even better day. Their dreams would help to keep the Revolution alive; their vision would help to insure that the state of South Carolina would not be an exact replica of the colony.

Epilogue

On August 5, 1776, the independence of the United States of America was proclaimed in Charleston. At twelve noon the town regiment of militia was drawn up under arms in Broad Street. Forty-five minutes later President John Rutledge, Major General Charles Lee and his chief subordinates, members of the privy and legislative councils, members of the lower house, and officers of the army appeared in a procession which halted at the front of the regiment. The Declaration of Independence was read. The procession then moved slowly east on Broad Street to the Exchange where the Declaration was read a second time. The multitude responded with cheers; the cannon at the bastions along the Cooper River with salutes. That evening the Declaration was read to the army encamped on the plain north of Charleston; and on the following day to the troops at Forts Johnson and Moultrie. "No Event," William Tennent noted, "has seemed to diffuse more general Satisfaction among the People. This seems to be designed as a most important Epocha in the History of South Carolina, and from this Day it is no longer to be considered as a Colony but as a State."

BIBLIOGRAPHY

ARTICLES

Calhoon, Robert M. and Weir, Robert M. " 'The Scandalous History of Sir Egerton Leigh,' " *William and Mary Quarterly* (Jan. 1969), pp. 47-74.

Greene, Jack P. "Bridge to Revolution: The Wilkes Fund Controversy in South Carolina, 1769-1775," *Journal of Southern History* (Feb. 1963), pp. 19-52.

——. "The Gadsden Election Controversy and the Revolutionary Movement in South Carolina," *Mississippi Valley Historical Review* (Dec. 1959), pp. 469-92.

——. "The Plunge of Lemmings: A Consideration of Recent Writings on British Politics and the American Revolution," *South Atlantic Quarterly* (Winter 1968), pp. 140-75.

Weir, Robert M. " 'The Harmony We Were Famous For': An Interpretation of Pre-Revolutionary South Carolina Politics," *William and Mary Quarterly* (Oct. 1969), pp. 474-501.

BOOKS

Alden, John R. *A History of the American Revolution.* New York: Knopf, 1969.

——. *The South in the Revolution, 1763-1789.* Baton Rouge: Louisiana State University Press, 1957.

Brown, Richard M. *The South Carolina Regulators.* Cambridge: Belknap, 1963.

Drayton, John. *Memoirs of the American Revolution.* 2 vols. Charleston: A. E. Miller, 1821.

Gadsden, Christopher. *The Writings of Christopher Gadsden.* Edited by Richard Walsh. Columbia: University of South Carolina Press, 1966.

Greene, Jack P. *The Reappraisal of the American Revolution in Recent Historical Literature.* Publication No. 68 by the Service Center for Teachers of History of the American Historical Association, Washington, D. C., 1967.

———. *The Quest for Power; The Lower Houses of Assembly in the Southern Royal Colonies, 1689-1776.* Chapel Hill: University of North Carolina Press, 1963.

McCrady, Edward. *The History of South Carolina Under the Royal Government, 1719-1776.* New York: Macmillan, 1899.

———. *South Carolina in the Revolution, 1775-1780.* New York: Macmillan, 1901.

Morgan, Edmund S. *The Birth of the Republic, 1763-1789.* Chicago: University of Chicago Press, 1956.

Ramsay, David. *The History of the Revolution of South Carolina From a British Province to an Independent State.* 2 vols. Trenton: Isaac Collins, 1785.

Rogers, George C., Jr. *Charleston in the Age of the Pinckneys.* Norman: University of Oklahoma Press, 1969.

Sellers, Leila. *Charleston Business on the Eve of the American Revolution.* Chapel Hill: University of North Carolina Press, 1934.

Sirmans, M. Eugene. *Colonial South Carolina: A Political*

History, 1663-1763. Chapel Hill: University of North
Carolina Press, 1966.

Wallace, David D. *The Life of Henry Laurens.* New York:
Putnam, 1915.

_____. *South Carolina, a Short History, 1520-1948.* Columbia:
University of South Carolina Press, 1969.

Wallace, Willard. *Appeal to Arms: A Military History of
the American Revolution.* New York: Harper and Row,
1951.